Elisa is a published author and researcher of psychic phenomena and has also written fictional horror and spiritual poetry. She is active locally and supports several charities. Elisa enjoys doing her oil paintings and tapestry work as well as reading. She spent several years in America where she lived in South Dakota and became a great friend of Del Iron Cloud, a Native American Indian who is a renowned artist in the Dakotas.

I dedicate this book to my late uncle, Mr William Jacques.

Elisa Wilkinson

BEFORE AND THROUGHOUT WWI AND WWII TO THE PEACETIME OF THE PRESENT DAY

AUSTIN MACAULEY PUBLISHERS™

LONDON • CAMBRIDGE • NEW YORK • SHARJAH

A CIP catalogue record for this title is available from the British Library.

ISBN 9781528994828 (Paperback)
ISBN 9781528994835 (ePub e-book)

www.austinmacauley.com

First Published (2021)
Austin Macauley Publishers Ltd
25 Canada Square
Canary Wharf
London
E14 5LQ

My husband and I have lived in our present home at Thornes, Wakefield, for over the past sixty years. Our youngest daughter passed away when she was only ten years old from disseminated lupus. But our surviving daughter Lesley Anne who has fought against the same crippling disease that took away her sister is quite an entrepreneur.

Along with running her own thriving foot care business in Harrogate, North Yorkshire, Lesley, Anne also works with her father doing most of the secretarial work for our businesses in both England and abroad.

I myself am a published author and I write mostly about psychic phenomena, ghosts, poltergeist, UFO, and investigate any form of phenomena that is occurring at the present time.

We do however talk about the past members of our families and this is what inspired me to write this book. My late uncle, Bill Jacques who lived at Preston Lancashire did not have many visitors except for my daughter and myself, therefore we used to travel to Preston to visit him once a fortnight.

During our many visits, he used to tell us of some of his experiences during the 2nd WW and gave me a photograph of himself receiving an award from the Dutch burgomaster and the resistance fighters. It is due to his courageous deeds that I was inspired to write this book and I dedicate my book to his memory.

I wish to thank my cousin Linda Elliot, who lives in South Africa, for sending me some of the photographs of her father, Bill Jacques, 2nd WW.

I thank my husband's cousin Mrs Doreen Wilson (nee Lawson), who lives in Scarborough, for the photograph of her dancing with her father William Lawson (1st WW Veteran) and her mother, Mabel Lawson, playing the piano in a dancing competition in Paris 1956. Plus, the photographs of her uncle Henry Behrens. The world's smallest man, he was William and Mabel Lawson's brother-in-law.

A collection of my own photographs.

Cyril Rowe 1st WW.

Herbert Farnsworth 1st WW.

Bill Jacques 2nd WW.

Bill's wife Jessie Jacques 2nd WW.

Mabel Lawson, with her nephew Eric Wilkinson.

Ken Wilkinson RAF after 2nd WW with Steve Davis and the cup commemorating him.

Eric Wilkinson.

Mr Alkesh of Photopoint Ossett, for enhancing the photos for my book.

Table of Contents

Preface

My book consists of a number of events that occurred before and during the 1st and 2nd World Wars (WWs) and up to the present time.

In parts, you may find the odd story amusing, although other events are rather disturbing and have left such devastating memories in the mind of the person involved in the atrocity of war that they are now unable to speak about them.

It is sad to say that there were many valiant men and women who gave their lives for their country's freedom. Some, however, by an odd stroke of luck, were fortunate enough to survive the horrors of the war and returned home to their loved ones.

Others who were given no option and were ordered to stay behind to destroy anything of value to the enemy, and to fight with what was left of the enemy, were unfortunately killed.

These forgotten men who were left behind had to fight, and struggled desperately for survival; they also had to find their own way home from foreign lands alien to them. In many cases, their relatives received a telegram from the War Office announcing that they were missing in action and presumed dead.

Cyril Roe, 1st WW Veteran

Cyril Roe was a gentle, retiring man, who never had any family of his own due to the horrendous injuries he received after shrapnel almost severed his leg. Because of the injuries he received to his legs and the lower extremities of his body, he broke from his fiancée telling her that she could not marry half a man. Although she argued about his condition, he was adamant and told her to find someone whom she could marry and bear his children.

Nevertheless, he was always surrounded by children. He taught many youngsters how to play chess, snooker and how to create wonderful carved figures and boxes. He was a close friend of ours, and my husband and I still have the two boxes that he made for us as wedding gifts. We always regarded him as part of our family.

Cyril Roe with Ken Wilkinson, my husband's brother, who later became a snooker champion and played against Steve Davies.

Cyril Rowe with my late brother-in-law Ken Wilkinson

A Life Ruined by War

In 1914 Cyril was called up into the army where he saw plenty of action that he wouldn't speak of, although he did tell us of how he came to lose his leg in the war.

At the time, he and a group of soldiers were fighting for their lives after suffering heavy losses and defeats when being constantly bombarded by enemy guns and cannon fire. They were struggling desperately to survive in knee-deep sludge, water, and filth, with rats scuttling around them, and the stench from the rotting corpses of dead soldiers who had lost their lives in the disease-riddled trenches in France.

Keeping their heads down low, the soldiers tried to find as much shelter as they could in the filthy trenches, but many brave men lost their lives when flying shrapnel exploded all around them.

Cyril was one of the men who was unlucky enough to be caught by shrapnel that almost lacerated his leg when it sliced through his knee. It also caused him other devastating injuries.

Bleeding profusely, one of his comrades tied a tourniquet above his wounds and blew a whistle in the hope of gaining a medic's attention over the constant pounding of gunfire. In the meantime, Cyril had to wait in excruciating agony, along with the dead and other wounded men, until the firing eased so that the medics could get through to them.

By now Cyril was lapsing in and out of consciousness and when the medic reached him and cut away his clothing, it revealed the horrendous wounds to his body. It was clearly visible that the worst of his injuries were on the lower half of his body, and from the knee down his leg was just a mangled mess of tissue that was being held together by a piece of skin.

Therefore, as the bombardment was so heavy and they couldn't get him back to the field hospital, the medics had no option but to amputate what was left of his leg right where he lay.

In the filthy trenches without any anaesthetic, the medics gave him something to bite on so that he wouldn't bite off his tongue and amputated his leg, then tended to his other life-threatening injuries; otherwise he would have bled to death and died in the rat-infested trench.

In the meantime, dodging bullets and bombs, the brave stretcher bearers managed to get him to the field hospital to have his wounds properly cleaned.

It was too late, however, as the filth and poisonous bacteria from the trenches had already begun to invade his wounds and within a matter of days, gangrene set in.

Due to this Cyril had to undergo a further amputation, and when he was deemed of no further use to the army and well enough to travel, Cyril was sent back to his home in England and released from the army with an honourable discharge and provided with a prosthetic leg.

Before the war, Cyril had a fiancée who loved him dearly and upon his return, despite his disabilities, she still wanted to marry him, even though he said that in the foreseeable future he would become a burden to her and broke off the engagement.

He purchased a detached house at the edge of Thornes Park, Wakefield, where he taught children living in the neighbourhood how to carve objects from wood, especially wooden boxes with secret drawers. He also taught them snooker, and chess as well as many more intellectual games, whereby all of the children would flock to his home to learn various crafts.

My husband and his brother were two of the children who gathered there.

Christmas was the only time that I can recall Cyril leaving his home, and that was when he came to our home for his Christmas dinner and played chess with Eric in front of the roaring fire.

Due to what was termed as modernisation, the council compulsorily compulsory purchased his home and moved him into a bungalow for retired people on Thornes Road. From that day on, Cyril appeared to lose heart and resigned himself as being no use to society and became a recluse and stayed there until the day he died a sad and lonely broken man.

Shortly afterwards, the council removed the remaining tenants from their bungalows, and demolished them and sold the land to a housing developer. They also demolished the old school behind the bungalows that Mrs Gaskell had provided for young children to be educated.

On the site of Cyril's old home, the Council built a bungalow for any of the ground men that were employed by the council, that came along to take care of Thornes Park.

There is no respect for the young and the elderly when it comes to profit.

John Hellier, 1st WW
My Husband's Grandfather

John Hellier, from Shepton Mallet in the Cotswolds, worked on his father's farm. However, due to him having so many brothers, there wasn't enough work for them all whereby John left the farm and travelled to Yorkshire to find work.

It didn't take long for John to find a job on a farm in the local area, due to him being experienced with horses and cattle. He trained horses to work on the land and in his spare time he rode and helped to train the race-horses for the local racetrack. This was how he acquired the nickname 'Jock'. In 1914 John saw the outbreak of the 1st WW, and was enlisted along with many others to fight the enemy. He was, however, one of the many number of men who would not speak about the atrocities of war that he had witnessed, but he did speak of one amusing incident that occurred when he was in France.

At the time, due to the heavy fighting, John and a small attachment of men who had been cut off from the main battalion, had run out of food and were almost starving. They had managed to survive between skirmishes on raw vegetables dug up from the land and whatever liquids they could find that were clean enough to drink. The water however, mostly came from the streams they were lucky enough to come across, that wasn't contaminated by dead people and animal carcasses.

One day, as they were approaching the ruins of a bombed farm, they stopped before going any further to discuss briefly what they should do. Knowing that the enemy was usually lying in wait in the bombed ruins to shoot any stragglers or unsuspecting troops when they tried to take shelter from the bullets and shrapnel flying around them.

After a brief discussion of what they should do, the men cautiously surrounded the wrecked building. After giving it a thorough search, they found that it appeared to have been abandoned by its owners sometime earlier, so they stayed inside for a short while waiting until the coast was clear before moving on. At that time, the men had hardly eaten or drank anything for days, their stomachs ached and their throats were parched and burning, so John volunteered to go outside and search for the water trough that the animals drank from. He knew there should be a well and a pump to obtain fresh water for the animals and proceeded to search for it.

But when he eventually found the well, he discovered that it had been blown to pieces by the heavy shelling. There were also the corpses of what John presumed to be, were of the farmer, his family, and some of his workmen floating amongst the debris. Cursing his bad luck, John began searching about the farm hoping to find something edible to eat and drink, but there was nothing.

Whoever else had been there before them had taken everything with them when they had fled from the approaching enemy army.

However, when John heard a strange sound coming from the barn directly ahead, he immediately took cover. When for a few brief moments he stayed where he was holding his breath and not daring to move, then realised that it was the sound of an animal in pain. His first instinct was to put the beast out of its misery and drew his knife, then staying alert for any traps that may have been laid, John carefully edged his way inside the barn and gave a huge sigh of relief when he saw a cow standing there with a full udder almost begging to be milked.

Being a farmer, John knew exactly what to do: he grabbed a pail that was nearby and began to milk the cow. He then took the bucket full of warm milk to his buddies, who cheered when they saw him approaching with the cow following close behind.

The men had plenty to drink that day and for a few more days after, as the cow stayed with them. Sadly though, it ran away when a heavy bombardment of shells landed close to them.

John said, "That cow was a lifesaver," and he was sorry to see it go.

William Lawson 1st and 2nd WW Veteran and the Angel of Montz

William and the Two World Wars

The 1st WW

In 1914 William was enlisted to fight in the 1st WW. At the time William was dug deep in the filthy trenches at Belgium fighting for his life along with many other brave men who were struggling to stay alive. As the bombs and shrapnel burst all around them, William and the other men who were aware of the mutilated and dead soldiers lying alongside them, could hear the heart-rending cries of the injured and dying above the din of the bombs landing close by, when suddenly a miracle occurred.

In the midst of the battle, the most amazing phenomenal sight of an angel appeared hovering between both fighting factions. Within seconds, all soldiers ceased fighting on either side and gazed in awe at the incredible being. Some soldiers dropped to their knees, bowing their heads and crossing themselves, while others were mesmerised and stared open-mouthed wondering what it could mean.

They then realised that it was Christmas and the angel was telling them that she was a symbol of peace.

This sighting was to become known as the Angel of Montz, Belgium.

Throughout many difficult times, and seeing many of his comrades die in appalling conditions, William managed to escape unscathed from every danger and returned home in 1918.

He said that it was not only the bodily injuries that many men suffered from, but like himself, it was the bad psychological problems that arose afterwards. Where the horrific memories and dire situations of what had occurred out there had risen and flooded their minds.

William Lawson 2nd WW

In 1939, William was again called up to fight in the horrors of another war. He was, however, classed by the younger generation of troops as being one of the old men, as the forces were filled with much younger men. Nevertheless, the government was willing to sacrifice anyone for their own means and were taking boys as young as 14 and 15 as well as the older generation.

William wouldn't talk about what occurred during his time in the forces, but the only experience he would speak of was when they were rescued at Dunkirk.

He told his daughter Doreen, that those who could swim were ordered to swim out to the ships and board them, while those who couldn't swim had to wait in queues to be picked up and were slaughtered where they stood by enemy aircraft fire.

When they were climbing the rope ladders that were thrown over the sides of the ships, he said that countless numbers of men were shot from the ladders as they tried to board the ships and their bodies were left to the ravages of the sea. This was something he would never forget and that the horrendous memory haunted him to his dying day.

After his rescue, William was shattered and couldn't take anymore fighting, so he was sent to Scotland where he and his wife Mabel along with their young daughter Doreen went to live until the war was over. He said that it was so peaceful there it was hard to believe that the country was at war.

William Lawson in the
Years of Peace

William Lawson was a very astute businessman. He opened one of the first dance halls in Wakefield at the Wakefield Corn Exchange, where he held weekend dances. This later became a roller skate rink. The man whom he employed as a bouncer at the time, was one of his friends, an ex-policeman, Mr Dane, who came from a family of fully trained police officers.

William also opened and started dancing classes at the Criterion Ballroom in Wood Street Wakefield.

To add to his creative abilities, William decided that the dance floor needed glitter and he came up with the idea of sticking silver paper onto a spherical globe above the dancers heads to give character to the hall. This idea was taken up by someone who eventually prospered from William's original creative invention, by adding mirrors to the sphere.

The Corn Exchange where William Lawson opened the dance hall, was a beautiful old building with huge Corinthian columns and carved features. However, due to the defective decisions made at the time by the Labour Council to have the historic building demolished, many people believed that this was to be the start of the destruction of Wakefield as a historic city.

How right they were. William's wife Mabel Lawson played the piano for him wherever a dancing event was held, he was also a professional judge of many dancing competitions and travelled across the country judging these events. He later moved to Bridlington, East Yorkshire, where he opened a school, teaching ballet and tap dancing.

One young boy whom he trained won the first prize for tap dancing on a large drum. His daughter Doreen was also a trained ballet dancer and appeared in shows at the Spa Theatre in Bridlington, where Mabel accompanied the dancers by playing the piano.

Mabel also played the piano and organ for the silent movies, she also started one of the first ladies' bands in England.

Mabel Lawson

William Lawson's wife, Mabel was a very talented lady; she played the piano for the Ivy Benson band and helped to form one of the first ladies' bands in England, but had to leave to take care of her baby daughter Doreen.

Some years later Mabel started her own ladies band where they played at the Esplanade, Bridlington. She also played piano for many of the stars who performed there. The Esplanade was later to become known as the Spa. She also played the piano and organ for the silent movies, and became renowned for the various instruments she could play.

Mabel was an extremely talented lady.

William Lawson (WWI veteran) dancing with his daughter Doreen in a dance competition in France; his wife, Mabel who was an accomplished pianist is at the piano.1956

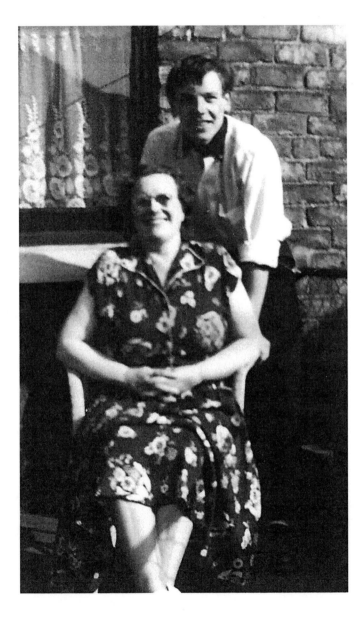

Mabel Lawson with her nephew Eric Wilkinson

Henry Behrens

The Smallest Man in the World

William Lawson's sister and brother-in-law toured the world during the 2nd WW entertaining our troupes and the public, also when peace was declared.

Heinrich Behrens, who altered his Christian name to Henry, was also known by his stage-name as Henry the 1st King of Lilliput, he stood only 30 inches tall and weighed 2st 4lb, and was deemed to be the smallest man in the world. Henry and his wife Emmie, known as Pem to her close friends and relatives, were said to be the smallest married couple ever known and toured the world exhibiting their famous act (Music in Miniature) with Burton Lester's midget troupe.

A sad incident occurred while appearing at Bertram Mills circus when Henry and his wife were injured after being trampled by performing elephants that stampeded after a dog that should not have been on the premises began barking at the elephants and frightened them.

After a lengthy court battle, Henry successfully sued Bertram Mills circus.

Throughout their lifetime, Henry and Emmie toured the world entertaining people with their music and other entertaining acts.

When finally returning to England, Henry and Emmie began appearing at the Grand Theatre Leeds, where Henry had a huge cat named Blackie that used to pull him around in a cart that was specially designed for him. It was during many of his excursions about town, that he was stopped by many of his admiring fans who wanted his autograph, therefore being a congenial man, Henry always had the time to stop and sign their autograph books and to chat with the people.

Some years later, however, Henry's health began to deteriorate so he retired and went to live at Flamborough East Yorkshire. He next moved to Cardigan Road, Bridlington where he sadly passed away.

The photographs are my own and were given to me some years ago by Henry's niece Doreen.

But our favourite photo is the one of her uncle Henry with Stan Laurel and Oliver Hardy.

THE SMALLEST MAN ON EARTH
60 years of age, 30 inches high, and 32lb. in weight

THE SMALLEST MAN IN THE WORLD, 30" HIGH, 32LBS. IN WEIGHT, 60 YEARS OF AGE

THE WORLD'S SMALLEST
MARRIED COUPLE

The World's Smallest Married Couple
and Famous Cat Blackie

Blackie was the cat who pulled Henry in his specially
designed cart.

HENRY BEHRENS,

Height 30ins. Weight 32lbs. Age 56 years, with his wife, Emmie, in their Famous Act "Music in Miniature," on returning from their Sensational World Tour.

Henry and Emmie played a large variety of different musical instruments. All of the instruments they played were designed to measure to their size.

Henry with Stan Laurel and Oliver Hardy

Herbert Farnsworth
1914–18 WW

Herbert Farnsworth, my late grandfather

Before the 1914–18 war, Herbert lived on Providence Street in Wakefield with his wife and children where he ran his own green grocery business.

His warehouse was situated on Brook Street, opposite the old market, that used to be a thriving prosperous concern. Unfortunately, the market that was the lifeline of Wakefield no longer exists after its demolition in the 1960s and the warehouses that used to span the length of Brook Street have now gone.

Regrettably, the warehouses have now been developed into shops.

At that time, Herbert had a stall on Wakefield market from where his produce was sold. He also used to travel around the area of Wakefield with his horse and cart selling fruit and vegetables door to door.

Sadly though, Herbert's family and business life were ruined by the outbreak of the 1st WW and he had to say goodbye to his wife and children after being called up for military service.

He would never speak of the atrocities that occurred during the fighting, but one of his daughters told me of his valiant attempts to escape after being captured and imprisoned in a Russian labour camp, where many of the men died after being repeatedly tortured and starved to death by their inhuman captors. They were forced to march through knee-deep and freezing cold snow, mud, and icy conditions to reach the prison camps, where under violent intimidation, they were put to work for the Russian cause.

Nevertheless, during his interment there, Herbert always tried to escape on his wife's birthday, but he never made it back to safety and was always recaptured.

After his first bid for freedom, he was caught, beaten and flogged to within an inch of his life by the sadistic Russian soldiers, but he didn't, however, let this deter him and he tried again the following year, only to be recaptured when he was hampered by the deep snow. Upon his capture he was beaten and taken to a place of punishment, where this time they stripped him naked and tied his feet and hands together and slid a long pole beneath the ropes to hoist him up onto two beams. They then pulled back his head and pushed a tube down his throat and force-fed mustard gas directly into his lungs.

Despite the appalling torture, Herbert made numerous attempts to escape only to be recaptured, beaten and force-fed the mustard gas again and again.

This horrific, barbarous cruelty was carried out on a regular basis by his inhuman Russian captors as part of the punishment and as a warning to the other prisoners who were considering making an attempt to escape.

From being a fit and healthy businessman, who like many other people that were forced to join the army, they were returned home either crippled or mentally confused.

Herbert after his liberation was stretchered back to England, a bodily wrecked and broken man, with a collapsed lung and tuberculosis in the other. He was taken to Ilkley Moor Sanatorium, a convalescent home to help him recover from his wounds before being allowed to go home to his wife and children.

When he did finally return to his family, his wife Harriot who had been informed that he was dead, and had been receiving a war widow's pension of two shillings and six pence per week was hanging out the washing and nearly collapsed with shock when he arrived home.

She had not been informed that he was alive, and did not recognise him, as he had lost so much weight and grown a beard.

The insensitive hard-hearted government, however, insisted that she pay back every penny of what she had received of her widow's pension after Herbert had been pronounced dead.

From my memory of my grandfather, he was always cold and constantly spat blood into the fire where he huddled to keep warm.

For his long painful suffering, and him leading valiant attempts to escape from the prison camp, Herbert was awarded the victory campaign medal, and a silver watch, which was presented to him by Col. Sir E.A. Brotherton Bart, MP for Wakefield. He was also given a horse and cart to resume his business.

However, after only a few years of working, the horse slipped on the tramlines in the Springs in Wakefield and broke its leg and the poor animal had to be shot.

Not to be deterred, Herbert bought another horse at an extremely reasonable price named Satan. When Herbert first saw the horse, he took a liking to it because of its frisky manner and shiny black coat, although he was curious why the man was selling it so cheap as the animal appeared to be fit and well, but he was told by the owner that the animal was vicious.

Therefore no one wanted him because of his bad attitude, it would bite and kick if anyone got too close and he was considering sending it for slaughter.

Herbert thought for a short while as he studied the beast, that he couldn't let the animal go for slaughter, the animal was too young. The horse was also fit and healthy, so he decided to buy it. Gradually with patience and the understanding of animals, Herbert spent as much of his spare time as he could with the horse and managed to tame it and they became good friends.

However, in time the horrendous punishment he had received in the war caught up with him and he was forced to retire. None of his sons wanted to carry on with the business so he sold everything.

Herbert died on 14 July in Clayton Hospital, Wakefield, just a few years later.

A patronising, patriotic gift of medals can never replace a healthy mind and body.

Herbert Farnsworth is at the centre of the photo,
in the first row.

1659/D/KOY.

CERTIFICATE of*
~~Discharge~~
~~Transfer to Reserve~~
Disembodiment
~~Demobilization~~
} on Demobilization.

HOME DEFENCE

Regtl.No. 20077 Rank. PTE.

Name in full ...... FARNSWORTH. HERBERT.
(Surname first)

Unit and Regiment or Corps }
from which   4 K.O. YORKSHIRE L
~~*Discharged~~
~~Transferred to Reserve~~
Enlisted on the...... 28ᵀᴴ OCTOBER 1916.

For ...... K.O. YORKS ......
(Here state Regiment or Corps to which first posted)

Also served in ......

......

Only Regiments or Corps in which the Soldier served since August 4th, 1914, are to be stated.
If inapplicable, this space is to be ruled through initial and initialled.

†Medals and }
Decorations   NIL
awarded during
present engage-
ment

*~~Has~~
~~Has not~~ served Overseas on Active Service.

Place of Rejoining in }
case of emergency   ...... Medical Category ......

Specialist Military }
qualifications   ...... Year of birth 1889

He is*
~~Discharged~~
~~Transferred to Army Reserve~~
Disembodied
~~Demobilized~~
} on 11ᵀᴴ April 1919

...... in consequence of Demobilization.

...... Signature and Rank.

Officer i/c ...... Records. ...... YORK (Place).

w* Strike out whichever is inapplicable.   † The word "Nil" to be inserted when necessary.

(20996). Wt. W 8211—P.P. 2329. 3,000m. 1/19. D 10 &. (E 1256.)

BUCKINGHAM PALACE

1918.

The Queen joins me in welcoming
you on your release from the
miseries & hardships, which you have
endured with so much patience &
courage.

During these many months of trial,
the early rescue of our gallant Officers
& Men from the cruelties of their captivity
has been uppermost in our thoughts.

We are thankful that this longed
for day has arrived, & that back in
the old Country you will be able
once more to enjoy the happiness of
a home & to see good days among
those who anxiously look for your
return.

George R. I.

The letter from King George to my grandfather upon his release
from the Russian prison of war camp.

Below is the watch he received from Councillor Brotherton.

Herbert's wife, my grandmother Harriet Farnsworth, has a plaque commemorating her at the LGI hospital in Leeds. She was the first person to receive gold injections against cancer.

She also gave a home to many of the Spanish refugees who fled from Spain during the Spanish Civil War.

Herbert Farnsworth's son, Sam Farnsworth, was my father.

Sam is the 4th person on the front row of the photo

Sam joined the RAF, but as he was afraid of height and couldn't carry out the parachute jumps, he was placed in the RAF Military Police, where he became a sergeant.

During his tour of duty in London, like many others, he wouldn't talk of what occurred there. He did however tell me of one horrific incident that he could never shake from his mind.

The Buzz Bomb

One evening, when it was time for a shift change at the munition factory, and hundreds of people had finished work for the day, as the day shift workers were leaving the factory gates and the night shift came on, one of the first German buzz bombs flew overhead. As no one had ever seen one of these weapons before, they were totally mesmerised and unaware of what danger they were in, and what damage the bomb could cause. Therefore, the crowd of people stopped walking and stared upwards watching and wondering what would happen. Within seconds the bomb became silent, then dropped, the explosion was ear-shattering and bodies flew through the air in all directions.

Sam recalled that a woman's body flew straight past him and landed on thick cast-iron spiked posts, where she was impaled and died before anyone could help her. Some were torn to shreds by the force of the blast and others, who only a few minutes earlier had been fit healthy people, were now crippled, blind and deafened. While others who were suffering from appalling injuries lay on the ground missing limbs, struggling to get to their feet without realising they had no legs.

Many who survived without injury were left almost naked from the force of the explosion, as it had torn most of their clothing from their bodies, while others staggered about in shock, not knowing what to do, and could not understand what had happened. Sam said that the people who were able to help did try to give assistance to those who were seriously injured.

This was just one of the vicious cruel acts that were implemented during the war on innocent civilians that was meant to break their spirits. But the enemy was wrong, they couldn't break a true Englishman's courage.

Sam did, however, say, that this first horrendous atrocity was the one he would never forget.

The Brave Airmen

Another bad time was when the fighter aircraft returned, many of the crew were either injured or killed, but the worst sight of all was the shattered undercarriage where the gunners had been. Sam wouldn't say any more.

An Amusing Incident

Late one night when Sam was on duty in London, he arrested a man who was drunk and shouting obscenities in the street. He arrested him and took him to the police station where the police locked him up for the night. That man was JAMES MASON, the film actor.

Prisoner of War Camp, Stanley Hill, Wakefield

Some years later, Sam was transferred to Yorkshire where he was put in charge of guarding the prisoners of war at the detention camp situated at the top of Stanley hill near Wakefield where a mixture of Italian, German, and others, were detained until the war ended.

His main concern however, was that the prisoners who were allowed out for a period of time to work on local farms throughout the day. They carried concealed flick knives, and if approached, they would use them on innocent civilians.

The Bible

When out on patrol one day in London, Sam found an American Air Force pocket-sized Bible in the street. He kept it as a souvenir from the war and my mother gave it to me some years later. I would like to return the Bible if possible, to the man's family somewhere in America or Canada. If by some chance that person's relatives are living here in England and could possibly recognise the name. Then I would be more than happy to return the Bible to its rightful owners.

But I must have positive proof and identification before I will hand over the Bible.

Attention

By special request of the U. S. Military and Naval Authorities you are instructed to place your NAME ONLY on the fly leaf, *nothing more.* On no account name your organization, post, ship or station at any place in this book. To do so might afford valuable information to the enemy.

A Sacred Token

To *Richard C. Downey*

From *Chaplain Vincent E. Nelson*

_____

_____

_____

Date

THE WHITE HOUSE
WASHINGTON

January 25, 1941

To the Armed Forces:

As Commander-in-Chief I take pleasure in commending the reading of the Bible to all who serve in the armed forces of the United States. Throughout the centuries men of many faiths and diverse origins have found in the Sacred Book words of wisdom, counsel and inspiration. It is a fountain of strength and now, as always, an aid in attaining the highest aspirations of the human soul.

Very sincerely yours,

Franklin D. Roosevelt

Franklin D. Roosevelt.

Bill Jaucqes' 2nd WW

These true accounts entail the remarkable courage of a remarkable man, my uncle, Mr Bill Jacques from Wakefield West Yorkshire, who was ordered to stay behind in a foreign country with his men and destroy whatever he could that would be beneficial to the enemy. This included weapons, fuel, food, that had been abandoned or dropped by the unfortunate soldiers who were gunned down by the enemy on the beaches at Dunkirk.

These men, who were left behind at Dunkirk, were forced to undergo a strenuous struggle for survival. Despite all of the odds being stacked against them, Bill did manage to return home some weeks after the war was declared over.

This is Bill's Story

Bill's life was disrupted in the 1940s by the outbreak of the 2nd WW, where he saved a countless number of lives in Northern Europe. He survived being shot a number of times but managed to scramble to safety. He survived Dunkirk and was safely on-board ship with his best pal Jock where they were ordered to return to land and blow up ammunition dumps, set fire to the cornfields and destroy anything that could be of any value to the enemy.

When Bill's family received the dreaded cold-hearted telegram stating that he was missing in action and presumed dead, Bill's mother refused to believe it and said, "They can't kill our Bill," and she was right, they couldn't.

But first, I will give you, the reader, an insight as to what Bill was truly like. At six feet tall and muscular, due to all the sports he played, Bill majored in all sports – cricket, swimming, tennis and rugby.

In the 1930s, he played rugby for Hull Kingston Rovers, but at the time his entire life's ambition was to win trophies for the cricket club he played for, Paton and Baldwins Sports Club at Thornes Wakefield. Here he worked as a lorry driver for Paton and Baldwins, transporting wool to various depots around the country.

Paton and Baldwins Mill that stands on Denby Dale Road, Thornes, Wakefield, is still in use but not as a mill as we knew it. The Mill was closed down many years ago and now the whole area has been swamped with small commercial businesses.

Bill was also an avid motorcyclist and when the confines of work were over, he would get on his treasured second-hand BSA motorcycle and enjoy the sensation of freedom that he loved, when feeling the wind blow on his face as he sped along the winding country roads of West Yorkshire.

Another of his strong ambitions was to ride and own a Harley Davison motorcycle, which he believed would pull the girls.

It took many years, plus many harrowing experiences, before he would have the opportunity to achieve his heart's desire, but when he did, it was short-lived.

Bill's Cricketing Years

From a very early childhood, Bill was a cricket fanatic. His father enjoyed the sport and whenever possible he would take young Bill along to whatever match was being played.

There are two plaques at Lawfield Lane School, Wakefield, where Bill was the vice-captain of Cricket and Rugby at the school.

He also did a test period with The Yorkshire Cricket Club.

Bill's favourite sport, however, was cricket and as he progressed throughout the prevailing years with the game, his skill with the bat and fast bowling was finally recognised by Paton and Baldwins Cricket club. Whereby the organisers asked him to join their team, where he proceeded to help them win many cups and trophies.

Bill is the 4th man to the left on the back row.

P. & B.—In unforgetable memory of the day when WALTON slaughtered PATONS & BALD- WINS at College Grove, July 17, 1948.

When we are old and turning grey,
Someone is surely bound to say,
" Remember that match at College Grove,"
When Walton put us in a groove? "

Ramsbottom did the fine trick.
Of taking eight wickets (without his horses head stick),
And in P. and B's. room they played the harp,
For Handscombe, Cass, Brook and **Sharp.**

But who was that lad, for goodnesssake,
Oh yes, a batter called Billy Jaques,
Who wickets going with a bang,
Put on his pads and merrily sang,

Away to the wicket he strode with glee,
And still was batting when they stopped for tea,
Good old Billy, now we must win,
And drink out of the Cup at the Commercial Inn.

Clarry polished the table and ordered the tea,
For those dashing men from Patons and B.
But Walton said " No, we,re taking the Cup,
For we get thirsty and would like a sup.

Again to the wicket, the hope of his side,
Went young Billy Jaques to turn the tide,
And as time went on in his eyes came a glint,
For in Eastmoor Road, the lamps then had lit.

Knowing his side to be in a fix,
Delighted the crowd with a mighty six.
Even Clarry, the Capt., was heard to say " Whew."
If we don't win to-night no Brentlea Avenue.

But now I must come to the end of the tale.
It was a pity that Patons did fail.
They tried so hard in a sporting fight.
That lasted well into Saturday night.

A Poetic Tribute to Bill Jacques

Bill is the 6th person standing on the back row.

He played for Paton and Baldwins Cricket Club at Thornes sports ground. You can see the railway arches in the background connecting the mainline from Leeds to London.

THE WAR YEARS 1939–1945

Bill is the 4th person on the back row at an unknown country
manor, where the men were stationed and trained before
leaving the country.

During the 2nd WW, all branches of the Armed Forces
commandeered many country houses and large hotels to house the
troops.

If anyone recognises any one of the soldiers in this photograph
from the 171 Coy RASC Armed Brigade, I would be grateful if
they would contact my publisher.

Debriefing for soldiers by an unnamed man from the War
Ministry, before being sent to fight in North-West Europe.

Bill is the man wearing helmet No. 81

Bill was a dispatch rider with the 171 Coy RASC Armed Brigade and a trained survival expert in life-threatening situations. He rode a BSA motorcycle carrying vital messages from the army headquarters to military units. As well as this, he travelled ahead of the convoy on the lookout for the enemy.

Bill, along with many others, was sent out to Northwest Europe to fight in the 2nd World War, where many of the valiant men lost their lives, the main loss being at Dunkirk.

In his years in the army, Bill worked his way up the ranks and became a Lance Corporal where he commanded his own elite group of men.

There were numerous times, he said, that many soldiers were half-starved and froze to death where they stood when the stormy winters snow covered the ground and the harsh unrelenting winds cut through the clothing tightly wrapped around their icy cold bodies.

These weather conditions made it almost impossible to push forward and gain ground from the enemy. When at times, some of the artillery guns froze up and gave them no cover at all from enemy fire, leaving them defenceless as the ground was too hard for them to dig into.

France

Although reluctant to speak of the incidents during the war, I did manage to cajole him into telling me and my daughter Lesley of some of the horrendous events out there. These were confirmed by his daughter Linda, who lives in South Africa.

One incident Bill recalled was one winter's evening when out on patrol with his closest friend, Jock, riding their BSA motorcycles, they had approached a road that narrowed considerably and had slanted slopes and thick foliage on either side. To Bill, this was the ideal spot for an ambush and he was right, there were two bodies lying in the middle of the road. Whereby without any hesitation their natural instincts took over. Both men slowed their bikes to a halt and rolled into a ditch at the side of the road, drew their guns and lay in wait, expecting at any moment to hear German voices approach, but none came.

Laying on their bellies, Bill and Jock kept their heads down for a while and waited before cautiously lifting them and peeped through the long grass. Where they saw up ahead in the fading daylight two American soldiers lying in the road, who appeared to be dead. He also saw two German soldiers sprawled halfway down an embankment. They were lying in such awkward positions there was no mistaking that they were also dead. It looked as if the Americans and Germans had shot one other. However, not wanting to take the risk of being shot, the two men instinctively stayed where they were and scanned the area expecting someone to have heard the sound of their bike engines, but everything remained silent.

After waiting for a considerable length of time, and with it becoming dark, Bill decided that the coast was clear and told Jock to stay where he was for the time being. Bill carefully made his way first to the Germans to check they were dead. He next checked on the two Americans and found they were also dead and signalled for Jock to join him.

Bill then turned his attention to the two Harley Davidson bikes lying on the road. Bill had always wanted to ride a Harley, it was his dream machine and he knew that if he didn't chance it now, he would never get the opportunity to ride one again. Despite the grim events that had transpired, Bill went over to his own bike and pushed it into the hedge bottom. Then, after ensuring that it was well hidden, he went over to the two Harleys and picked one up, started it and rode away with Jock riding shotgun on his BSA.

Bill's joy however, was short-lived when his commanding officer ordered him to return the Harley to its original owners, the Americans, he ended up riding another BSA.

"At least I had ridden a Harley," he said later.

France

A disturbing incident occurred one dark stormy night when on patrol in France. Bill, along with three men, Jock, and two others, were met by a sobbing terrified child, who in broken English and part French managed to make them understand what the problem was. There were four Russian soldiers attacking the child's mother and sister in the nearby farmhouse, and her father had been beaten and was tied up on the floor with his head covered in blood.

Bill managed to pacify the girl and told her that they would help but for her own safety, she should stay where she was.

After working out a plan of strategy and keeping close to the hedges for concealment, Bill and his men crept steadily forward until they reached the farmhouse and peered in through the window. Here they were met by the appalling sight of the child's mother and her eighteen-year-old daughter who had been stripped naked, who were being raped by the soldiers.

Taking the Russians by surprise, Bill and his men smashed the door open and fired a volley of shots into the air, then at gunpoint they forced the enemy soldiers to stand by the wall. Jock untied the man on the floor, who was stunned and bleeding heavily from head wounds, which he had received from a vicious attack when he had tried to protect his family.

By now the women were screaming and had become hysterical, but Bill managed to calm them and ushered them out of the kitchen, along with the farmer, before turning his attention to the rapists. Bill and his men forced the Russians to strip at gunpoint, then after tying them up, they calmly sat down and smoked a cigarette, chatting to one another loudly on what punishment they should administer to the brutal soldiers.

Then after finally making their decision, Bill called the family into the kitchen and whispered something to the teenager.

A look of surprise crossed over the girl's face, then with a wry smile Bill, and her family, marched the naked Russians outside, where Bill handed the girl his gun. Without any hesitation, despite their pleas she shot the four rapists dead.

There are four rapist enemy soldiers buried on land somewhere close to a farmhouse in Northern France, where they won't be carrying out any more atrocities against innocent civilians ever again.

Belgium

Despite shells bursting all around him, and him dodging bullets from enemy weapons, Bill kept his head low as he raced on his trusty BSA motorcycle across bumpy tracks of land to reach the main base.

At the time, the road was covered with huge potholes where bombs were dropping and creating huge depressions which was making it dangerous for anyone to travel, especially for the troop of English soldiers, who were following a few miles behind on foot and in vehicles.

Therefore, to reduce the danger of falling into one of these craters, Bill had found it easier to travel in the ruts across the fields where the ground was more even. Nevertheless, he was on open ground and in danger of being shot, so whenever possible, Bill would try to find another route that wasn't quite as exposed.

However, in the distance he had noticed something that gave grounds for concern. When seeing a German soldier sneaking towards a group of British soldiers, whose attention was solely in one area where the Germans were attacking, Bill knew that the enemy never travelled alone, so there had to be more of them nearby, neither had they heard his motorbike approaching because of the artillery shells exploding around them. Taking advantage of the noise, Bill ditched his bike and moved swiftly towards the German, then drew his knife as he crept close and came up behind the enemy. He was about to dispose of him when he heard someone from behind ordering him in German to halt and put up his hands.

Bill knew that he didn't stand a chance of getting out of there alive as it was two to one, so instinctively, Bill did what he had to do and pushed the dead German away from him. Then not dropping his knife, he turned with his hands held high in a gesture of surrender.

Filled with outrage at seeing a fellow soldier killed, the German officer ordered Bill to drop his weapon. But knowing that he would be defenceless if he did so, Bill refused, so the German shot Bill in each arm expecting him to drop the knife.

Bill felt the hot searing pain as the bullets went straight through both arms and winced at the agonising pain. Yet Bill stood his ground knowing that it was now a matter of survival, it was either the German or him. Bill felt the adrenalin race through him and before the German had another chance to fire, Bill was on him and the enemy dropped to the ground fatally wounded.

Bleeding heavily from his wounds, Bill carried out what he had been ordered to do and staggered back to his bike to ride back to his company, and to relay the message from headquarters to base that a massive German unit was moving towards them.

He spent the following two days in a military medical tent recovering from his wounds before returning to duty.

Due to his bravery and heroic action, Bill saved the lives of hundreds of British soldiers and for his outstanding courage and bravery, he was awarded a certificate of Merit from Field Marshall Montgomery.

SANDAL SOLDIER AWARDED
CERTIFICATE OF MERIT. —
Lance Corporal W. Jacques, of 17,
Pugneys Road, Portobello, serving
with the R.A.S.C. (Armoured
Brigade), has been awarded the
Certificate of Merit. It is signed
by Field Marshal B. L. Montgomery, Commander in Chief of
the 21st Army Group, and reads
as follows:—"It has been brought
to my notice that you have performed outstanding good service
and shown great devotion to duty
during the campaign in North-
West Europe. I award you this
certificate as a token of my appreciation, and I have given ins ructions
tions that this shall be noted in
your record of service."

Bill's award for bravery from Field Marshall Montgomery.

21st Army Group

T/157562 L/Cpl W. JACQUES

171 Coy RASC (Armd Bde)

It has been brought to my notice that you have performed outstanding good service, and shown great devotion to duty, during the campaign in North West Europe.

I award you this certificate as a token of my appreciation, and I have given instructions that this shall be noted in your Record of Service.

B. L. Montgomery

Field Marshal
Commander-in-Chief, 21st Army Group

Date_____ 4 FEB 45 _____

Dunkirk

Dunkirk will be remembered as being one of the biggest massacres of men and women who fought in the 2nd WW, where the defence and evacuation of the British and Allied forces in Europe took place at the battle of Dunkirk from 24 May to 4 June 1940. This battle saw 1,600 of our own servicemen callously mown down by German bullets and slaughtered on the first day.

The German pilots flew low, allowing their gunners to butcher hundreds of servicemen and women who had no chance of survival. Whereby the troops had nowhere to run for cover on the open beaches and the sea, and were easy targets for the German gunners. Although they found it sickening, many of the soldiers were forced to take cover beneath the bodies of their fallen comrades in the hope of avoiding being shot.

Bill remembered seeing the bodies of men floating all around him in the water who couldn't swim and had drowned, yet had waded out to sea in the hope of avoiding being shot. He said they queued neck-deep in the sea for almost two hours awaiting rescue, fully expecting to be the next casualty. Only small boats could get close to the beaches, as most of the vessels were too big and heavy and would have run aground if they had got closer to the shore. Therefore, the crews on the big ships could only watch in frustration, helpless and desperate at the sight of the troops being cut down and massacred without mercy.

Owners of fishing vessels, private boats, yachts, pleasure cruisers and other smaller craft from all over Britain, volunteered to rescue the stranded men and sailed out to help in the rescue. Unfortunately, they weren't immune to the bombs and bullets that flew around them and despite their heroic efforts, many of these small boats were hit and sunk before they could carry the soldiers to safety.

Jock, Bill's closest friend, couldn't swim and was shorter than Bill, but Bill hung onto him and held his head above the water until they were finally rescued.

When the rope ladders were thrown down over the sides of the ship, Jock was trembling from the coldness of the sea and his hands had turned blue with cold.

"I can't get a grip," Jock groaned each time he tried to climb the rope ladder. Instinctively Bill offered to help, then unexpectedly Jock let out a loud scream and shot up the ladder.

Bill laughed when he said that he had grabbed Jock's courting tackle, and squeezed, that was how he got Jock aboard the ship.

That wasn't the end of it for the others though, for as the troops were climbing the rope ladders hanging over the sides of the ships, the German pilots brought their aircraft in low, allowing the gunners to shoot the men who were struggling to escape from the chaotic mayhem, sending their bullet-riddled bodies falling over the men who were struggling to climb up the rope ladders, back into the freezing cold sea.

Bill said it was horrendous and once aboard the ship, everyone took cover where they could, thanking their lucky stars that they were still alive.

However, once aboard the ship, the commanding officer asked for volunteers to return to the land to blow up and destroy anything that could be of value to the enemy.

"I want you, you and you," he said pointing to Bill, Jock and Harry, to go back and destroy everything that can be of any use to the enemy. I want you to blow up the heavy equipment left behind by the troops, blow the ammunition dumps, burn the fields, and kill every animal in sight.

"Now look what you've got us into," Jock moaned.

"It's because you're so bloody big and look as if you know what you're doing, that's why he chose us."

After a hushed briefing with the commanding officer, the three men were bundled into a small launch, and fitted out with extra supplies of food and ammunition. They were then navigated a short distance away from the heavy fighting, and landed in a secluded cove. From where they landed to set about the arduous task of destroying the abandoned vehicles, weapons and ammunition by blowing them up and setting fire to them.

They next made their way inland to sabotage ammunition dumps, contaminate water supplies and destroy fields of crops. Sad to say the farm animals, cows, poultry, abandoned pets had to be put down, otherwise they would have provided food for the enemy. Everything that the enemy could have used was destroyed. With Bill, Jock, and Harry being left behind at Dunkirk, and nothing being heard regarding their safety. After a period of time, the war ministry proposed that they were dead, and sent telegrams to their families saying that the men were presumed missing and killed in action.

Unknown to them though, the three men were carrying out missions that were so highly confidential even most of the top brass were unaware of what was going on.

However, when Bill's mother received the dreaded telegram from the War Office saying that Bill was dead, her first reaction was, "They can't kill our Bill."

She ran to her husband's place of work to tell him the bad news.

Although stunned, he agreed with his wife and asked for leave from his job, which was refused.

(To this day I would love to know the name of that company and expose them for what they were). Nevertheless, Bill's dad walked away from the job despite being threatened with being sacked.

Bill, in the meantime, had carried out every order he had been given. Harry had been killed by enemy gunfire, leaving behind him and Jock, lost and alone in a foreign land, and having to fight their way back to the coast.

Nevertheless, despite being wounded and filthy and the odds stacked against them, especially when coming across the odd German soldier, who like them was sick and tired of the killing, acknowledged one another and went their separate ways.

Yet regardless of the difficulties and dangers that arose, Bill and Jock did finally manage to reach the coast. Where they acquired rides from friendly Dutch fishermen in their boats, who were only too pleased to help them.

They were then changed from one fishing boat to another, until they were in the English Channel, before being handed over to English fishermen who brought them safely home.

Filthy, exhausted and bedraggled they arrived at a railway station where Bill borrowed two pennies from a sergeant major, to make a phone call to someone who knew his parents, letting them know that he was still alive.

It was rumoured among the survivors of Dunkirk sometime later, that at the time of the mass slaughter of defenceless men and women on the open beaches and in the sea. That ships laden with valuable works of art, relics and bullion was being safely shipped from Dunkirk without any trouble from the enemy, yet leaving men and women behind to suffer such appalling deaths.

The big question is, WHY?

Why was it, that the Germans were allowed to cut down and assassinate so many people at Dunkirk?

It was the opinion of many of the surviving men of Dunkirk, that it was a mass murder arranged by unnamed people in positions of power, to distract the public's attention away from what was really occurring there.

There is an old saying, "Human life is the cheapest commodity you can get."

Bill did say that when it came to Christmas, the British, and German troops, stopped fighting.

They exchanged beer, cigarettes, food and chocolate with one another and even had a friendly game of football. Then when the Christmas period was over, they shook hands and went their separate ways.

The Ultimate Insult

An extremely offensive incident occurred a few weeks later when Bill and Jock were at a bar having a relaxing drink. When a foreign drunken sailor turned to Bill and Jock and said in a sneering tone that he could drink four beers and four whiskies faster than you, lot came out of Dunkirk.

Jock asked the man to repeat what he had just said.

The drunk opened his mouth to speak, but not before Jock head-butted him in the face and put him on the floor saying.

"That's how fast we came out of Dunkirk."

The bar dropped silent and nobody said a word and carried on drinking, leaving the drunk to be carried out by his shamefaced companions.

Bill's Sister

In the meantime, Bill's sister died after suffering from cordite poisoning while she was helping the war effort by filling bullets and cartridges for use in the 2nd WW ammunition factory.

She suffered an agonising death, along with many other women and men from the cordite poison, which caused their entire body's eyes and fingernails to turn yellow and hair to fall out. Bill never forgave the Ministry for her death.

Arnhem

Bill received many more wounds during the war, on separate occasions he was shot in the chest and the legs while saving the lives of others. He also endured watching his fellow soldiers and friends die. And when his troupe was cut off from the rest of the battalion, and were close to dying from hypothermia and starvation, Bill kept them going, he did everything in his power to encourage the soldiers to survive.

His biggest achievement, however, was at Arnhem.

At that time the Germans had taken control of most areas of Holland and the situation had become extremely tense.

When the British arrived at a village in Arnhem, they were appalled at the destruction there.

The whole town had been reduced to rubble by the constant bombardment from both German and British artillery. Not one building was left intact and almost everything was raised to the ground In between the bombardments of the town, however, there was a half-hour lull, whereby within minutes Bill had put forward a plan of action. He asked if anyone was still alive and hiding in the ruins, but was told that all of the people had fled the area.

Bill had however noticed that part of the church was still standing and enquired if anyone was trapped in there. The top brass told him no. It was explained that the people had either fled when told that the Germans were coming or had been killed by the constant bombardment of the town.

But, Bill's instinct told him they were wrong, he had noticed that amongst the bombed-out ruins of the church, some parts of the building were still intact. He knew that the older people who could not escape or travel very far feared the threat of being tortured and shot by their captors and this terrified them. Therefore, the first place they would go for would be to the sanctity of the church in the belief that God would save them.

He told the commanding officers that if the church was still standing then it would be possible there could be survivors in the crypt. Bill asked that when the lull between the fighting came, if he and his men could go to the church and check to see if there were any people left alive in there.

The officers shook their heads.

"There's nobody left alive in there," he was told.

But Bill didn't agree and insisted that there would be survivors hiding in the crypt of the devastated wreckage of the church. In the end due to Bill's arguing and persistence the officers finally gave in and Bill detailed six men to go with him.

When Bill and the men got to the ruins of the church, they shouted down through the broken arches of the crypt, that they were British troops and there to help them. In an instant, they heard the pitiful cries calling wearily from the remaining inhabitants buried below, who were trapped and begging for help to be rescued from behind the fallen masonry.

Whereby, when discovering that there were still people alive beneath the ruins, Bill and the soldiers began digging at the rubble with their bare hands and didn't stop until they had made a safe route through. He then sent one of his group members racing back to the commanding officers to report their findings and asked for an army truck so they could get the people to safety.

But within minutes the Germans had begun shelling the town again and the soldiers had to run for cover. But Bill was determined to stay with the trapped people and he ordered the remaining men to return to the safety of the regiment. He then had an agonising wait until the German artillery halted bombarding the area.

Then, after the bombardment had ceased, the soldiers returned to the ruined church and began rescuing the survivors. The survivors were mainly elderly people, women and children who were very weak and exhausted, they'd had no food or fresh water for over a week, and had done the best they could to survive. They had managed to drag the bodies of those who were deceased, and had hidden their bodies away from the sight of the children into a dark recess of the crypt.

Bill said that the stench emanating from the corpses was appalling.

Nevertheless, disregarding the horrendous circumstances and accustomed to being surrounded by death, it took Bill's team hours between bombardments before everyone was brought to safety from the crypt of the ruined church.

One elderly lady would not let anyone touch her except Bill, who in her eyes was her saviour. She pointed to him saying (Icka, Icka), although I don't know if I have spelt it correctly.

There is a photograph by Pathe News and the Dutch resistance of him lifting the elderly lady from the back of an army truck, where both are smiling happily.

This is the lady whom Bill rescued amongst many others from the bombed church at Arnhem, that the top brass was going to leave behind to perish in the ruins.

Bill receiving medals and honours from the Dutch Burgomaster and the Dutch Resistance for saving countless lives at Arnhem.

AROUND THE CITY

Happy end to war tale

THE hunt for information about a Wakefield war veteran pictured in a Dutch newspaper has led to Lytham St Anne's.

Two weeks ago Isaac Creasy asked Wakefield Express readers if they could help him find out more about the unknown soldier.

Mr Creasy was intrigued after receiving a Dutch newspaper article from his son, who lives in Holland, featuring a wartime picture of a Wakefield soldier, "Korporaal Jacques," lifting an old woman from a lorry.

Mr Creasy's appeal was spotted by Mrs Elisa Wilkinson, niece of Bill Jacques, the man in the picture. She put the two men in contact and they have since spoken by phone.

"I really appreciated the piece that was in the paper," said Mr Creasy, of Pilmer Court, Lupset.

However, both are agreed that they never met.

Mr Jacques was a despatch rider with the 171st King's Own Yorkshire Light Infantry and his niece hopes to hear from former comrades who fought with him at Arnhem so she can put them in touch as well.

Mrs Wilkinson can be contacted on Wakefield 360826.

Bill was traced by the grandson of the lady that he helped to rescue from the bombed church in Holland.

Bill was surprised when opening the door of his home one day, to find a young Dutchman standing there wanting to thank him personally for saving his grandmother's life. Bill took him inside where they discussed the incident that led to the valiant rescue. The young man knew that despite the heavy bombing, Bill was the only one who stayed at the church giving hope to the women and children trapped there.

Bill said that it was something he hoped he would never have to do again, the scene was more than horrendous, and he couldn't put into words what he saw in comparison to the carnage and suffering there.

Bill relaxing at home in 1995. Whenever my daughter and I visited him at his home in Freckleton, Lancashire, despite the pain he was suffering, Bill always had a smile on his face.

Not only did Bill save the lives of men, women and children, he also rescued many animals that would have died if it hadn't been for him.

Bill was also involved in the battle for the Arnhem Road Bridge.

This was featured in the film 'A Bridge Too Far'.

Jock

The incident that really distressed Bill however, was when he and Jock were racing on their bikes along one of the deserted country lanes.

At the last moment Bill spotted a tripwire strung across the road and instinctively ducked shouting for Jock to get down, sadly Jock didn't hear him and was decapitated by the wire. This incident occurred six weeks before the last day of the war.

To the end of his life, even though he had developed health problems, diabetes and Alzheimer's, Bill never forgot Jock and would talk about him constantly.

Belson

On 15 April 1945, British troops liberated Belson. At that time Bill was one of the first men to enter Belson and was interviewed by David Dimbleby. He was, however, surprised to see how many Australian, American and other Europeans were imprisoned there along with the Jews.

Bill said that he didn't want to kill anyone, but once you were in the thick of the fighting it was a matter of survival. Kill or be killed. He was, however, a kind-hearted man who loved his wife Jess, whom he nursed for 22 years after she contracted Multiple Sclerosis. His daughter Linda sent me some of the photographs in my book from her home in South Africa, and authenticated all of the stories that Uncle Bill told me.

Armley Jail Leeds

After Bill was de-mobbed, he resumed working as a driver at Paton and Baldwins mill, but he found the job mundane and boring after serving such active duty in the armed forces.

Therefore, he decided to join the Prison Service, where, because of his exemplary conduct in the army and passing all of the necessary exams, he was soon accepted and began a new career as a prison officer at Wakefield, West Yorkshire, in 1952.

From there, in 1953 he went to Armley Jail in Leeds, in no time at all he was promoted and put in charge of C Block, this was the punishment block where the inmates were held for flogging and hanging.

Throughout his career, Bill worked alongside Albert Pierrepoint, the respected hangman, and said that in most cases the criminals received the punishment they deserved.

Those were the killers of elderly people, small children, unarmed police officers etc, anyone who was helpless to defend themselves. These people merited being put away from society for good.

He also said that eight out of ten who were flogged, said they would have committed a more serious crime if it had not been for fear of the death penalty.

What more can be said when the words are straight from the mouths of criminals.

Bill in his prison officer uniform.

Jesse Jaques, Bill's Wife
Bill's wife Jesse joined the WAFS and became a sergeant. Jesse
is seated on the right.

BEAULIEU

Jess was stationed at Beaulieu; she was standing along with a group from her squadron on the railway station at London when they saw one of their own aircraft shot down by an enemy fighter. Unbeknownst to Jess at the time, the pilot shot down was her first husband.

Jess in the centre of the photo; she was always happy
and smiling.

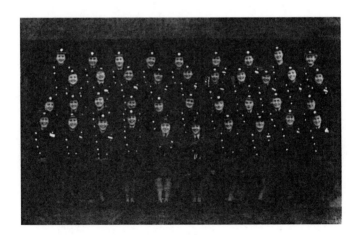

Jesse is the 3rd person on the left of the second row.

Comin' in on a Wing and a Prayer

Comin' in on a wing and a prayer
Comin' in on a wing and a prayer
with our one motor gone
We can still carry on
Comin' in on a wing and a prayer.

What a show what a fight
Boys, we really hit our target for tonight
How we sing as we limp through the air
Look below, there's our field over there
With our one motor gone
We can still carry on
Comin' in on a wind and a prayer.

Comin' in on a wing and a prayer
Comin' in on a wing and a prayer
With our full crew on board
And our trust in the lord
We're comin' in on a wing and a prayer.

Ken Wilkinson, RAF Peace Keeping Movement in Germany After 2nd WW

William Lawson's Nephew

In the 1950s shortly after the 2nd WW had ended, Ken Wilkinson from Holmfield Lane, Thorne's, Wakefield, was stationed in Germany as part of the peacekeeping movement. At that time, the Germans were constantly fighting the British troops who were still stationed in Germany. Whereby, as it was beginning to become a political issue, as well as a major problem for the British to control, it was also being published in the media.

In the light of this, the government decided to send a high ranking General to Germany to solve the problem and check on the army's efficiency.

At the time, Ken was a firefighter with the RAF in Germany.

When the General arrived, unknown to some of the men stationed there, he decided to give the camp and officers an exercise that entailed landing a plane in critical difficulties and all emergency staff be placed on full alert to deal with the emergency.

Whereby the whole camp was put on standby for the exercise, and when the alarm was given, Ken, and the fire crew were ready to deal with the emergency. Consequently, when the alarm sounded, Ken who was the driver of the fire engine, raced to the vehicle and jumped on board, and drove out on the double from the fire station.

Unknown to Ken however, the man in charge of opening the doors had not got the door high enough for clearance and as Ken drove out, the ladders and part of the equipment were torn from the roof of the fire engine.

Unsure of what to do, Ken kept going and drove alongside the plane dragging the ladders with him behind the unit until the plane stopped, then got out of the vehicle.

The sergeant who stood alongside Ken beside the stationary aircraft, was raging mad and told Ken that he would get three years jankers for this.

Nevertheless, when the general alighted from the aircraft, he looked at the firemen asking, "Who was driving the fire engine?"

The sergeant roared, "Step forward Wilkinson."

Shamefaced, terrified and shaking at his knees, Ken stepped forward waiting for the dressing down he expected. He honestly believed that he would be spending the rest of his time in the army jailhouse, and almost collapsed with shock when the General turned to him saying, "If I was in an emergency landing, then I hope that you will be driving the fire engine as you did what was right by not stopping."

Ken could hardly believe his ears and for once in his life he was struck dumb.

Some months later, when the General's batman retired, to Ken's surprise the General asked for Ken to become his driver and toured all over Germany to various camps, allowing the General to sort out the problems that had arisen there.

Ken was de-mobbed after three years of military service.

Ken went on to become a champion snooker player and played against Steve Davies.

Peace Time Events and Achievements After The 2nd WW

Ken Wilkinson and Steve Davies at a Snooker Tournament.

FREE PRESS SPORT

Tribute to snooker ace

Mrs Marion Wilkinson, the mother of snooker ace Mr Ken Wilkinson, who died earlier this year, is presented (pictured right) with the trophy which her son won three times in succession, by the chairman of the Bridlington and District Billiards and Snooker League, Mr Trevor Pearson. Mr Wilkinson is the only man to win the open trophy three times – he won it in 1984, 1985, and 1986. The winner of the Ken Wilkinson Memorial Shield Mr Mike Lucas is presented with the award (picture far right) by Mrs Deborah Jarvis, the wife of the league's treasurer.

Ken was the first man to win the open trophy three times. He won the trophy in 1984, 1985 and 1986. The shield on the right is the Ken Wilkinson memorial shield.

He also trained the first woman champion snooker player.

85

The cup bearing Ken's name that he won three times.

Eric Wilkinson, Owner of Ltd Casings, Ken's Younger Brother

Amusing and interesting memories from the past that I am certain some of the older generation will recognise.

Eric was lucky, he just missed being called up for National Service by a few months before it was abolished. In 1957 it began being phased out and in 1960 it was abolished altogether.

When Eric was 18 years old, his father Harold Wilkinson owned a potato business at Thornes, Wakefield, from where he supplied many fish and chip shops in the surrounding areas, and Wakefield market with potatoes.

Harold was so busy with the deliveries that he only had enough spare time to give Eric three driving lessons in his Humber car before sending him for his driving test.

At the time there was a crisis in Egypt, and all of the experienced commercial drivers had been called up into the army and this included Ken, Eric's older brother. This inevitably left the country with no delivery drivers, whereby the government allowed learner drivers to drive unaccompanied, and Harold told Eric to do all of the local deliveries around Wakefield in the Bedford TK wagon.

However, when it drew closer to Eric taking his driving test, he tried explaining to his father that although he had been driving the wagon for two years, he had only taken three driving lessons in the car.

By now though, Eric was a confident and an accomplished driver, who was carrying out deliveries in Halifax, Huddersfield, Leeds, and many areas scattered about Yorkshire. He also travelled to Lincolnshire to pick up loads of potatoes in the TK Bedford wagon with its wooden floorboards.

(May I add that some of the floorboards were missing and you could see the road below?)

However, when the time arrived for Eric to take the driving test, he found himself behind time and was running late, and didn't have the time to go home to get changed before taking the test.

But after ringing his father to explain the situation, his dad told him not to worry; he said, "You've had enough experience driving the wagon, so when you get in the examiner's car, all you need to know is where the brake is, just take your time, look confident and you will be all right," and that he would meet him at the testing station.

But when Eric arrived late at the testing station driving the wagon, his heart sank when he saw the look on the examiners face, who was already standing outside checking his watch waiting for him to turn up.

Eric's first thoughts were, *This is bad, he won't pass me for being late.*

To his surprise, however, the examiner asked, "How long have you been driving that wagon?"

Eric replied, "About two years."

The examiner shook his head saying, "If you have been driving that for two years, then you will be capable of driving a car," and passed him.

Fish and Chip Shops

Harry Ramsdens fish and chip shop situated at Otley Road Guiseley, was just a small wooden hut when it first opened in 1928, and in later years it was developed into a restaurant.

As it was holiday time and the restaurant was filled with visitors who often travelled miles by coach to dine there. The company found that they were running low on potatoes so they rang Eric's father. As it was holiday time and an emergency, Eric was sent to carry out the delivery to the restaurant, by showing that he was willing to interrupt his holiday, Harry Ramsdens became customers of ours for many years.

Sammy Herbert's, Fish and Chip Shop, Kirkgate, Wakefield.

Eric also supplied Sammy Herbert's fish and chip shop in Westgate, Wakefield, opposite the old ABC Cinema, where he used to get lots of trade after the films were over, The ABC cinema has now been closed due to the American style, overpriced cinemas opening in Wakefield.

Sammy had a great sense of humour; he had his own insignia stamped on the cutlery used in the restaurant that read. (Stolen from Sammy Herbert's).

One day when Eric was making a delivery to Sammy, he heard him cursing and shouting in the back room at his son-in-law who was helping him to prepare food for the evening trade.

The man helping Sammy had poured a half hundredweight sack full of dried peas into the bath then filled the bath full of water. Whereby the peas had swollen and overflowed onto the floor.

Sammy was furious his profit was going down the drain fast and could do nothing about it.

Sammy had always soaked just a small amount of dried peas in a bathtub full of water to make them swell, they were later cooked for serving with the meals.

Another time after Eric had made his delivery of potatoes and stood eating his fish and chips, a man complained to Sammy that he had found a bone in his fish.

Sammy said, "Have you got a penny?" and held out his hand.

The man replied, "Yes," and gave him the penny.

Sammy said, "Thanks, I didn't charge you for that," and slipped the penny into his pocket and carried on with his frying.

The man was speechless and left without an argument; everyone knew that you couldn't win an argument with Sammy Herbert.

Local Election

In the late 1970s Eric stood for election with the Social Democratic Party and won many seats. However, due to his popularity, many undesirable occurrences began happening around us, and after numerous warnings and life-threatening events he was compelled to stand down.

Nevertheless, despite all odds and unforeseen setbacks, Eric has built up a thriving business from both of our premises, one at Green End Lane, Thornes Wakefield, and the other at Thorne's Lane Wharf, Wakefield. We have business dealings that cover England, Germany, Asia and Africa.

The Pool

In the 1980s we were sitting beside the swimming pool in Spain talking to a couple from London, who had a young baby that had just learned to walk when our conversation was suddenly interrupted when we heard when someone screaming that a baby had fallen into the 6ft deep end of the pool.

For a few seconds everyone appeared to freeze and didn't move; Eric however, even though he was unable to swim, without hesitation leapt into the pool and rescued the baby before sinking to the bottom of the water.

A man who had been watching dived into the pool and got Eric out before he drowned, Eric received many congratulations and thanks from the staff and almost everyone staying at the hotel.

The baby's parents never thanked Eric who risked his life for rescuing their son, nor did we see any of them again. We and the guests staying at the hotel presumed that they had returned to London.

Nevertheless, for the rest of our holiday, Eric was treated as a hero.

Eric with his fleet of vehicles

Eric has always been a hard-working man who will help anyone if the cause is genuine.

Harold Wilkinson, Eric And Ken's Father

In the early 1930s Harold hated working in the pit at Sharlston, Nr Wakefield, and welcomed every day when he didn't have to go down into the black depths of the coal mine to work long hours in dangerous sweltering or freezing waterlogged conditions.

After seeing what was happening to many of the older men who were working there for most years of their lives, Harold decided that he had had enough, he wanted to spend his life in the daylight and fresh air not in a dingy black hole, where at times the men had to struggle through water that was almost knee-deep and infested with rats.

Therefore, he left the pit and started his own business on Wakefield market selling fruit, vegetables, rabbit, chickens and eggs.

On his days off however, Harold would try anything to make extra money for his growing family. Whereby, when he discovered there was to be motorbike rally on Denby Dale Road, Wakefield, Harold knew that many people would be there as it was a hot summer's day, so he drove his old van to the ice cream makers and filled it up with ices to sell at the show.

In those days the ice cream came in oblong blocks and was wrapped in a greaseproof paper that was kept cold with dry ice.

(When enclosed between two wafers it was known as an ice cream sandwich.)

Due to the weather being so hot, Harold did a rip-roaring trade and by lunchtime he had sold all of the ice cream and customers were asking for drinks to cool themselves down.

With a bit of quick thinking and ingenuity, Harold went along to the local farmer from where he bought his fruit and vegetables in the nearby community, and asked one of the farmers if he could borrow a milk churn filled with water, that he would return later that day.

(The milk churns were made of solid steel and kept the milk cool.)

The farmer knew that he could trust Harold and filled one of the churns with ice-cold water.

Harold thanked him and went on his way. He sold the water for a penny a cup and was sold out in no time at all. The milk churn was made of steel and was very heavy when full, but Harold being the entrepreneur that he was didn't want to miss a sale.

He went back to the farmer numerous times to refill the churn, and by the time the day was over, Harold said that his efforts had made him a week's wages in one day.

On other occasions, Harold used to get the job of emptying railway wagons full of coal. In those days the coal wagons were emptied by hand and the men had to use shovels. This was hard work, so Harold paid half of his earnings from the job to pay others to do the back-breaking work.

In the late 1930s Harold had started his own Potato business and was building up a good round when he was conscripted into the army, therefore one of his brothers who was classed as unfit for the forces ran the business for him while he was away.

Nevertheless, when Harold returned home, he carried on and built up a thriving business until he was disabled and too ill to carry on, and passed the business on to Eric.

Whether it is in war or peacetime, all of our family members show that they will not be beaten by whatever obstacles that are placed in our paths. Our past relatives and ourselves are achievers, as my husband, daughter and myself still are.

The A Bomb

I do have an interesting little tale to tell and that is – some years past when my daughter and I were touring through Cornwall, we stayed at a small hotel overnight, where we met an American, who told us that he was one of the pilots who dropped the atomic bombs over Nagasaki and Tokyo in the 2nd WW.

None of the pilots knew who had dropped the live bombs, as some of them were duds. The reason being was that the pilots would not know who had killed and maimed so many innocent women and children.

However, over the years he said, that some of the pilots began developing a heavy guilt complex that resulted in them taking their own lives.

(In Nagasaki 39,000–80,000 were killed, and in Hiroshima 90,000–140,000 died, internet information)

The Japanese had refused to surrender, therefore it meant the heavy loss of troops of every nation if the war with the Japanese continued. Whereby this was the reason for the bombs being dropped over the cities. The Japanese surrendered a few days later and the war was declared over.

Sir Matt Busby, Manchester United

When Eric and I were flying to Monte Carlo, the man seated opposite me took out a cigarette and proceeded to light it. I did point out to him that there was a warning light saying no smoking.

He glared at me and put out the cigarette, but after a few moments he took out another, whereby I slapped his hand and told him to put it away until after take-off, which he did.

His wife, who was seated beside him, leant forward and mouthed the words to me, "Thank you."

However, when I glanced over towards him, I noticed that he was shaking and leant over the aisle to ask him if he was afraid of flying as he appeared to be extremely nervous.

He replied, "Have you ever been in a plane crash?"

I said, "No," and asked if he wanted me to hold his hand until after take-off. He nodded yes, and let me hold his hand while his wife held the other until we were airborne.

It was then that he introduced himself to me: it was Sir Matt Busby whose plane crashed in Munich, Germany on 6 February 1958, where many of his team, the Busby Babes lost their lives; Matt was one of the 21 survivors of the plane crash.

Both he and his wife thanked me for helping him on both the take-off and the landing of the aircraft.

Recalling Happy Memories

The stories before and after the war consist of amusing incidents and happy memories for a number of the older generation.

The younger generation do not know that at one point of time you did not have to take a driving test to get a driving license.

Older people will recall going to Sammy Herbert's fish and chip shop after a visit to the ABC cinema that was situated halfway down Westgate Wakefield.